The Educator as Manager

by
William E. Webster

SHAPIRO LIBRARY

Library of Congress Catalog Card Number 88-60068
ISBN 0-87367-273-9
Copyright © 1988 by the Phi Delta Kappa Educational Foundation
Bloomington, Indiana

This fastback is sponsored by the Wayne State University Chapter of Phi Delta Kappa, which made a generous contribution toward publication costs.

Table of Contents

Introduction

There is overwhelming evidence that organizations having a critical mass of high performers are better organizations. They are both more efficient and effective and have higher morale. In the private sector, profit margins are greater; and in the public sector, morale is higher and the employee turnover rate lower. In schools where there is high-performing leadership, achievement scores are higher and dropout rates are lower.

This fastback has been designed for educators who want to learn about the characteristics and activities of high-performing managers. It synthesizes the ideas of several experts on business management performance and includes examples of highly successful educational managers whose work I have been able to observe over the years. The ideas presented here are influenced by my own experience as well as by interviews I have conducted recently with effective managers in the public and private sector.

This step-by-step guide with questionnaires and personalized forms is intended specifically to help busy school managers analyze their current management style and to compare it with the styles used by effective organizational leaders. It also briefly presents a comprehensive strategy that educational managers can adapt in whole or in part for improving their overall management performance.

For purposes of brevity, the term "high performer" will be used throughout the text to refer to effective managers in a variety of settings.

Characteristics of High Performers

High performers are people who have high expectations and high standards for themselves and others. They have a personal mission that meshes with the organization's mission, and that personal mission serves as the driving force in meeting their own expectations and in carrying out every activity they perform. It is belief in the importance of their mission from which they derive their enthusiasm and excitement, which they in turn communicate to others. Fundamental to their activities is the belief that the key to a good organization is people — people who are effective individuals as well as contributing team members.

A principal in the South Bronx had as her personal mission the improvement of instruction and learning. In a school where both areas left much to be desired, improvement was clearly needed. In another instance, a director of special education in a large high school district in California, after visiting several classrooms, concluded that too many teachers believed that youngsters with exceptional needs were incapable of learning. The personal mission for these two managers was improved instruction. Their belief that instruction could be improved and their commitment to making it happen were the messages they communicated to teachers. They were not critical nor demeaning; but they made it clear that they truly believed that teachers could do better and that by working together, their respective organizations would improve. In both cases their missions and related activities motivated the staff to improve performance, which resulted in improved learning as measured by standardized tests.

High performers also have internalized a set of basic values with respect to their own integrity, honesty, and loyalty to the organization. They have a deep belief that they can perform better, that others also can perform better, and that their organization can become more effective through their better performance. They translate these beliefs into action in ways that others do not find threatening or intimidating but rather stimulating and motivating.

Such an individual was a superintendent of a large high school district in California, who realized that a high but stable dropout rate had become almost an accepted standard. He knew the long-term negative consequences that dropping out would have for a large number of students in his district, and he felt it warranted action on his part. Rather than confronting the dropout issue directly, which might have generated negative newspaper articles, he chose to move ahead on a variety of staff development activities, believing that better performance by district personnel could have a positive impact on the problem. Staff development included such activities as workshops on the use of classroom aides, teacher involvement in selecting new instructional materials, and staff exploration of the use of computers. Ultimately, his belief that the professional staff was capable of better performance paid off; within a five-year period and after much work and experimentation, there was a steady decline in the dropout rate.

Each person in the three cases cited, the inner-city elementary school principal, the director of special education, and the high school district superintendent, did a thoughtful analysis of past organizational performance before moving ahead. Each had some very clear ideas about what improvement activities were needed but recognized that the key people in the organization had to be involved in order for it to improve. And this improvement effort created a sense of mission not only for each of these three individuals but for a critical mass of key people in the organization.

Through words and actions, these leaders conveyed trust, admiration, and respect for the people with whom they worked. Their personal and professional commitments provided a sense of unity and direction for the improvement efforts, which was communicated to their staffs. All three believed strongly that teachers can improve, that youngsters can achieve more, and that schools can become a better place for students to work and learn.

A Checklist of Characteristics of High Performers

This checklist includes those qualities associated with high-performing managers as identified in the literature. How do you measure up?

- Are guided in all they do by strongly held personal and professional values.
- Have a singular sense of personal purpose, which becomes their mission for the organization; this purpose creates high expectations and gives focus and direction to all their energies.
- Understand that an organization can be improved only through the efforts of competent people working together.
- Have a strategy for regularly communicating the organization's mission to others, thereby generating systemwide commitment to the mission goals.
- Have a collegial system for monitoring progress on meeting the goals established by the mission.
- Stay in close touch with the people who do the work of the organization.
- Understand and accept that it is necessary to take risks if an organization is to innovate, improve, and meet the challenge of ever-changing circumstances.
- Stay attuned to the social, cultural, and political aspects of the environment that have an impact on an organization's operations.

- See themselves as teacher and motivator of their staffs; have their own program of training and self-renewal and encourage those who work with them to do likewise.
- Know the special skills and professional expertise of each person with whom they work.

Activities of High Performers

The Checklist of Characteristics of High Performers in the previous chapter provides a general description of the attributes and activities of effective managers. In this chapter we shall examine the specific activities of high performers, starting with the preparation of a mission statement. But a useful preliminary step to preparation of a mission statement is an inventory and analysis of your own core values — values that motivate you both on the job and in your personal life. (Use Chart #1 in the Appendix to record your core values.)

Personal Core Values Analysis

To see if your role in the organization is consistent with your deepest-held beliefs, you have to ask yourself tough questions in these three areas: 1) what you see as your personal/professional values, 2) what you see as your value to the organization, and 3) how the organization perceives you. Some questions you might ask yourself about personal and professional values might be:

- What is the purpose of my work?
- Why am I doing this?
- Who benefits from what I am doing other than myself?
- Where do such terms as honor, integrity, and courage fit into my personal value system?
- How do these values influence my commitment to my work?

- Where does my family fit in my life objectives?
- How do I balance family time and work time?
- What about community obligations that are not work-related?

Equally hard questions you might ask about your value to the organization are:

- What are my unique skills or competencies that help to make the organization more effective?
- How much time do I spend using these skills?
- What areas do I need to strengthen to become more effective?
- Am I an effective motivator; do I generate enthusiasm?
- Do my values communicate a tone of integrity?
- Do people understand my values; do they share my vision for the organization?

The third category, how the organization perceives my value to it, requires honest answers to such questions as:

- What signals am I getting from key people in the organization that tell me what my value to it is?
- Are my values consistent with the mission of the organization?
- Do performance reviews of my work focus on my true skills?
- Has it been suggested to me what areas I should strengthen, and are these suggestions consistent with my perceptions?
- Is there someone in the organization with whom I can have a frank discussion about my value and contribution to the organization?

On completing an analysis of your core values in these three areas, you can then begin to develop a personal mission statement. Obviously, the greater congruency between the values in these three areas, the more effective you will be in your organization. The three educational managers described in the previous chapter may not have gone through the value analysis as described here, but they surely must have felt they had great congruency in order to accomplish what they did in their respective organizations.

If, on the other hand, an individual finds that his values are not congruent with the organization's, then enthusiasm and commitment may be diminished and conflict is likely to arise. An experienced high school principal related the kinds of problems such incongruency can cause. When being interviewed for a new principalship, he was asked many questions about his knowledge of and experience with advanced placement classes and college admissions procedures, leading him to believe that the school was primarily a college preparatory institution. He got the job and assumed one of his values to the organization would be to strengthen the programs for higher-achieving youngsters and, equally important, to have the support of their parents. He was not long on the job when it became apparent that the percentage of college preparatory students was relatively small; there was a far greater number in the vocational and general curricula. Conflict with some of his superiors arose when he began to spend an increasing amount of his time working with the students and parents of the non-college-bound youngsters. One of this principal's core values was the belief that all youngsters in a school deserve attention and support, not just a handful going on to college. Because his superiors were responding to the highly vocal and well-organized parents of college-bound youngsters, they gave this group priority. And therein arose the conflict.

Developing the Mission Statement

A mission statement serves as the impetus for all the activities of the high performer. It sets goals and inspires actions that lead to innovation and organizational improvement. Imbedded in the mission statement are the carefully thought-through values in the three areas discussed earlier.

The mission statements of the three high-performing educators described in the previous chapter – the inner-city principal, the special education director, and the high school district superintendent – created the expectations, energy, and enthusiasm for their own performances and ultimately were accepted by those with whom they worked. They realized that if they were the only ones who had ownership of the improvement effort, it would fail. They recognized that it would take the combined efforts of everyone to make the organization work more effectively. Through their collegial style of operation, they made it clear that everyone was worthy of trust and respect. The mission was communicated to everyone through meetings, through discussions with individuals, and through communications with parent groups. They also took actions, such as bringing in outside speakers and initiating staff development programs. These high performers understood that it takes the personal commitment of everyone to give the effort unity and direction. By establishing group goals, they created the basis for both organizational and individual success.

It is crucial that individual missions be congruent with the mission of the organization. Conflicting missions can diffuse energies and create tensions. In one school district a rapid influx of Spanish-speaking youngsters generated enormous conflict. A majority of the staff believed that these youngsters initially should be taught in the language they understood, even if this required a crash training program for Spanish-speaking community members to serve as teacher aides. Others on the the faculty believed strongly in the traditional English-only approach; and therein was generated a sustained, debilitating conflict. In another school, without any staff involvement, a writing-across-the-curriculum program was launched, which generated anger and hostility on the part of math, science, and vocational education teachers who felt they were being asked to assume responsibilities that properly belonged to others.

In the first case, there was no leadership given as to what direction the school should take to educate non-English-speaking students. In the second case, a program was introduced that was resisted by a significant segment of the teaching staff. In each of these cases, time devoted to frank and open discussions about individual and organizational missions that best served the needs of all students could have avoided or at least lessened the conflict.

As the mission statement is developed, it is necessary to do a careful assessment of the current status of the organization. Since the mission focuses on the future direction of the organization, it is important to ask such questions as: "Are we doing better than we were two or three years ago?" or "Are there any areas where we do not seem to be doing as well?" The three successful managers cited above asked themselves these hard questions, and from this assessment they decided to launch their improvement efforts.

In developing a mission statement that is change-oriented (and most of them are), one can almost automatically expect opposition from those committed to the status quo. In any organization there are those who believe everything is fine the way it is and any change is tampering with the sacred. Often these beliefs are not based on any real data but are simply myths. The three educational managers cited had to deal with some of these myths; that is, children from an inner-city environment cannot learn; handicapped kids by their nature cannot learn; and the dropout rate has been about the same for years and cannot be changed. One of the key issues for each of these managers during the initial period of their improvement efforts was dealing with the inertia of the past.

A mission statement must have a clear focus. There is a tendency in writing mission statements to embellish them with flowery language and overblown prose. Keep the statement direct and simple. In a rural high school district with a high dropout rate, the staff decided to establish a program to deal with the problem. The program manager's mission statement was simple and right on target: "Bring back some of the youngsters who have left and develop strategies to keep those who are in school in school." In the private sector we have a good model of clear focus and succinctness in Lee Iacocca's mission statement. He said, "My mission is to save the Chrysler Corporation." That was good enough to get a two-billion dollar loan from the federal government. He did save Chrysler and paid back the loan.

It is important to put down your mission statement in writing. To put it in writing, you have to discipline yourself to compose a precisely worded document that communicates the importance and urgency of your mission. In addition, a written mission statement serves as a reference for measuring whether strategies to accomplish certain outcomes are working or whether they should be changed. Further, it communicates your goals and expectations to others, thus giving them a clear understanding of what they may be involved in.

Communicating the Mission

A high-performing educational manager makes sure the mission is communicated to the key players on the team, so they know where the manager is going and understand the yardstick to be used to measure progress.

Two cases cited below will underline the problems that can emerge where there is a failure in communicating the mission. A newly appointed principal was concerned because there was no system to measure instructional progress in her school. She set out to do something about it. At an early teachers' meeting she announced that in the future, as each teacher completed a chapter or unit of instruction, a test would be given and results reviewed by the principal. The principal's request to have current information about total class and individual student progress was not unreasonable. It could easily have led to staff discussions on what practices were working and where there appeared to be problems. However, the staff saw the new principal's demand as administrative interference and unnecessary surveillance, which called their professional integrity into question. The outcome was sullen compliance.

In the second case, a newly hired administrator of a large education agency informed his top-level managers at an early meeting that he was hiring a high-powered consulting firm to review management practices in the agency with an eye toward fundamental reorganization. Why he decided to move in this direction and what problems it was meant to address he never revealed. When the management-consulting firm's staff arrived on the scene and started conducting interviews, the agency managers expended enormous energy trying to find out the motivation of their new leader and supplied the interviewers with answers that would result in the least amount of change in the organization.

In each of the above cases, the leader's failure to communicate the mission, or by obscuring the mission, generated hostility and often covert opposition. In neither case was there any effort to involve staff in decisions. The mission may have been fully justified, but it was subverted because of lack of understanding and failure to motivate. Clearly, the staffs in these two cases did not see their leader's mission as their own. The mission that motivates high-performing managers also must motivate those with whom they work. It is important, then, in formulating a mission statement that it be reviewed and discussed with key people in the system. The mission might be altered somewhat as a result of the review; but with an opportunity for input, the staff would come to see the mission as their own and would work to see that it was achieved.

Reviewing Progress

As the staff works to meet the expectations of the mission, progress should be measured along the way. With agreement on the expectations and the yardstick for measuring them, assessment becomes a normal part of the process; and adjustments to the overall strategy can be made if the need arises. If the assessment process is to generate useful data, it will require the commitment of all in the organization. And they must feel free to report what is actually happening without fear of retribution or blame. The inner-city principal described earlier met periodically with grade-level teams to share successes and assess progress but also to identify problems. The high school district superintendent held monthly meetings to review progress on the dropout problem but also identified areas where there was lack of progress.

For the inner-city principal and the high school district superintendent, as well as the director of special education, the purpose of the assessments was not to point fingers at who erred or made mistakes but to find out how to do better in the future. With the focus on success, their staffs became committed to a program of change and improvement. These effective managers saw their role as one of creating a climate in which the involvement of key people increased the likelihood of meeting the mission goals.

Although each of the mission statements focused on improving teaching and learning, specific goals and expectations were changed. Most were met, but others were seen to be unrealistic. Sometimes the outside environment changed, creating new and different challenges. For example, in the case of the high school district superintendent, a rapid influx of Southeast Asian refugees caused him and his staff to undertake a major review of their dropout effort.

Staying in Touch with the People

Researchers who have studied high-performing managers report that effective managers spend a minimum of one-third of their time staying in touch with the key people in the organization. They suggest that an invisible manager is an incompetent manager. In a school context, these key people include teachers, aides, custodians, and cafeteria workers, among others.

By staying in touch with the key people in the organization, the high-performing manager can determine if the mission and the values it reflects have been communicated to others. For effective school managers, this means visiting classrooms, labs, shops, athletic fields, cafeterias, etc. One principal told me that he stays in touch by periodically following an imaginary student's schedule. An elementary school principal told me that she makes visits to all the classes in one grade to get a sense of what is going on at that grade level. Several principals have told me that they "wander around," but for a different purpose each day — one day a safety check, one day classroom instruction, one day student attitudes, one day discipline, one day pride in school. But in all cases the ultimate purpose of their wandering around was to assess progress toward organizational improvement. And they all reported that when someone made a suggestion for improvement, they made it a point to get back with a response to the person who made the suggestion.

The purpose of a mission is to give direction and a sense of cohesiveness to the work of others. By staying in touch, the high performer continually tests the validity of the mission. Along the way there may be defeats, disappointments, and surprises, both positive and negative. But by staying in touch and engaging in collegial decision making, the effective manager can redesign the mission so that it can be achieved.

Understanding the Changing Environment

Successful managers continually assess the nature of their working environment. Even though they may have little or no control over environmental changes, they see these changes as challenges to be met through innovation and new strategies. They accept the inevitability of change and, therefore, have plans ready to put into operation or on the drawing board when the need arises.

They are always alert to conditions that might have an impact on their organization's environment. For example, in the area of demographics, they anticipate how new industries in the community may create different demands on the schools. In one district the construction of a large semiconductor plant quickly changed the makeup of the student body. In another district the dramatic expansion of several defense-related industries changed the character of the community. In yet another district the bankruptcy of a major industry was immediately felt in the schools, with fathers unemployed and mothers going to work.

High-performing managers also are closely attuned to the actions of other agencies closely related to the schools, such as the central office, state government, and federal government. New demands for improved instruction emanating from many state capitals, sometimes in the form of exhortations but more often in the form of new mandates, have changed the way many schools do business. High performers recognize that they must be prepared to change as their outside environments change.

Parents also are an important part of the school's environment. Staying in touch with this important environmental component is a continuing task that effective school managers take very seriously. This process is a two-way effort: 1) communicating goals, strategies, and programs to parents and 2) assessing parental attitudes and concerns. A plan, then, for both parts of the process is important to the work of the high performer.

Serving as Motivator and Teacher

Through their actions, high performers become motivators. They understand that motivation requires action rather than exhortation. Their actions are consistent with the mission that has been previously reviewed and accepted by their colleagues. One of the inner-city principal's broad missions was improving her school's physical environment, with the immediate goal of reducing graffiti. To this end she took several concrete actions. First she talked to the teachers, students, and community members about how important an attractive and clean school is to effective learning. Then she arranged her own work schedule so she could inspect her building with the head custodian before school started each morning. She secured paint and paintbrushes from the school district's maintenance department, which at first was reluctant to give them to her because painting was the job of the maintenance department, not the custodian. But she persisted and was able to have the graffiti painted over before the students arrived at school. It was not long before the teachers, students, and parents became aware that the graffiti had disappeared; and they began to take pride in the appearance of their school. This principal changed how she managed the school, took some risks in bucking the bureaucracy, and by her actions communicated to the school and community the value of a clean and attractive learning environment.

High performers, by having their own program of training and self-renewal, motivate others to do likewise. A superintendent who recognized the growing importance of the personal computer as a management tool enrolled, and invited his immediate staff to enroll, in a series of weekend seminars sponsored by a nearby university. His example served as a visible motivation for others seeking training opportunities. The same superintendent also instituted a management training program designed to help administrators improve their performance, thereby enlarging the pool of high-performing managers.

Recognizing Colleagues' Special Skills and Their Value to the Organization

High performers know not only the special skills they themselves bring to the organization, they also know the special skills that others have to offer the organization. This includes teachers, custodians, clerical help, and parents. By knowing the special skills of every person in the organization, high performers can tap these skills to improve the effectiveness of the entire organization as well as to enhance the self-concept of those who are contributing their special skills for the good of the organization. Many high-performing managers keep a record of the special skills of persons in their organization. And they review and update them from time to time. (See Chart #2 in the Appendix as an example of a form for recording special skills and their value to the organization.)

In interviewing many school principals, I found that most of them had a good sense of the special skills that key members of their staff could contribute to staff development activities. For example, many of the elementary principals could quickly identify their most expert primary reading teachers and usually had on their records an indication as to whether these individuals were willing to share their expertise with beginning teachers. High school principals also could immediately identify their top writing and math teachers who, with some individualized training, could become valuable resource persons for staff development. The idea for Chart #2 came from these principals. The data on the chart also could be entered easily on a database system of a personal computer.

The Personal Work Plan

Although many school managers do not have a formal personal work plan or schedule, I recommend the use of such a work plan. The personal work plan is a self-disciplining technique to ensure that activities planned to accomplish the mission are carried out. It is a working document that includes goals, activities, and a time line. It serves as a point of reference when mid-course corrections are needed. The work plan establishes benchmarks by which to measure progress.

With a work plan a manager can develop a personal strategy to accomplish specific objectives within a designated time. Even when there are interruptions or crises (to be expected when running a school), the work plan helps the manager to get back on track. It serves as a personal monitoring system for charting progress or lack thereof. As goals are accomplished, the work plan may change; but the initial plan ensures that individual and organizational activities take place in a timely manner.

Assessing One's Time

A preliminary step in designing a personal work plan is to get an accurate and realistic assessment of how you spend your time. Estimates of time spent on certain activities seldom agree with actual time spent. For a week or two, keep a detailed account of what you do and for how long. Chart #3 in the Appendix shows how such an assessment can be made. It may show that a reallocation of time will be necessary in order to provide enough time for priority activities.

In addition to the detailed analysis of how one spends time provided in Chart #3, another type of analysis strategy is possible using Chart #4, "Improvement Activity Analysis." I first came upon this strategy after reading an article about how architects approach urban planning. Architects use a technique that they call pre-visualization. As they begin planning a new building, they visualize what the new building will look like, how it will fit in with existing buildings, and how it will change the city's or community's environment. I first began to use this technique while preparing for a fishing/camping trip. I carefully thought through everything I could see myself doing, such as finding the tent stakes, putting up the tent, assembling the camp stove, and other chores involved in setting up camp. I went through the same process in gathering my fishing gear, even down to putting on the waders, assembling the rod, tying on the flies, etc. After doing this several times, I found I left fewer things at home. I now go through a similar routine in planning and reviewing a week's work.

Using Chart #4 requires that you spend some time for both pre-visualization and post-visualization, focusing on three areas: self-renewal; improving individuals; and enhancing the organization, with an emphasis on improving teamwork. The first step is to visualize each day of the previous week, thinking very carefully about the activities you were engaged in on each day in that week. A date book or desk calendar is helpful in this step. Record the activities and time spent in the three improvement areas. Then visualize the upcoming week and identify the activities and estimate the time to be spent in the three improvement areas. By going through this visualization process for the past week and for the upcoming week, you are developing habits that contribute to a disciplined work plan.

Designing the Work Plan

As with the mission statement, a work plan should be written down. It should:

- Make clear what you are to do.
- Communicate to others what you are to do.
- Spell out the responsibility of others and provide time lines for completion.
- Serve as a measure of progress toward the mission.

The personal work plan (See Chart #5 in the Appendix) should include a brief restatement of the previously prepared mission statement, a listing of the goals or expectations to be accomplished during the week, a listing of the specific activities to be undertaken to realize the goals, a date for completion of an activity, and finally the results that are expected.

It is important to remember that a listing of goals is not set in concrete; the specifics of the work plan are always tentative and subject to change. But any changes should be thought through carefully and kept within the context of the original mission statement. And, of course, any changes should be communicated to those who are responsible for carrying out the activities. By developing a personal work plan, the high-performing manager serves as a model for others, who then can be encouraged to develop their own individual work plans.

Gathering and Using Data

Many experts on organizational management point out that high performers make effective use of data relevant to the mission of the organization. For schools such data might be standardized test scores, dropout rates over a period of time, or percentage of graduates going on to institutions of higher education. The effective manager must decide what data are important to collect and how they may best be used.

With key data presented in simple graphs (an easy chore with the personal computer), they can be duplicated and can serve as the basis for staff analysis and discussion. When data are gathered and presented in an organized way to staff members, there is an atmosphere for intelligent discourse among those responsible for the overall improvement of the school. Such graphs can be used as the basis for a "what-if" game. For instance, if graphs showing reading test scores showed no change over the past five years, what if they were to jump substantially in the next two years? What should the school be doing to make that happen? These graphs also can be made into transparencies for public presentations in the community.

A dynamic elementary school principal explained to me how she used data. In her first three years on the job, as a matter of routine she recorded the number of students referred to her for disciplinary purposes and categorized the referrals according to the type of infraction, noting particularly the referrals for fighting and truancy. At the end of the three-year period, she averaged the number of referrals for each month of the third year and for the two preceding years. Her data showed that the total number of disciplinary referrals, as well as the referrals for fighting and truancy, had been increasing gradually over the three-year period. At a before-school staff meeting in September, she presented the data and used them as a basis for discussion at that meeting and at several follow-up staff meetings. She also presented the data to parents. As a result of these meetings, the staff agreed to launch a school climate improvement effort to reduce the number of discipline referrals. The staff set goals for the next three years, and initial findings indicate that the program is working.

The superintendent of the high school district, whose mission was to reduce the dropout rate, started by collecting statistics from the previous five years. At the administrators' retreat before the beginning of the 1982-83 school year, he presented the dropout data for the previous five years and challenged his administrative staff to find ways to reduce the number of dropouts. At this initial meeting the staff participated in brainstorming sessions for ideas to attack the problem. And by early fall an overall district strategy was in place that allowed each of the district's 15 high schools to develop its own program for dealing with the dropout problem. During this period districtwide goals were set for each of the next five years. At the annual administrators' retreat, progress is reviewed and time is given for principals and other staff members to share their successes and to discuss all issues related to the district's dropout-reduction program. Each year a new dropout data chart is prepared to provide a focus for the discussions. These annual charts also are used for school board and community presentations.

The two examples cited above illustrate how data can be used to improve schools. High-performing educational managers know how to use data to accomplish their mission.

Conclusion

To be a high performer is not easy. The high-performing managers described in this fastback expended enormous energy and took considerable risks in order to achieve their missions. They were thoughtful and introspective. They knew how to use data to support their improvement efforts. But most important, they had a clear sense of their mission, which served to motivate them and those with whom they worked.

These individuals were action-oriented, but it was action executed with a plan. In carrying out their improvement efforts, they recognized that it was important to be sensitive listeners and to know the talents and skills of those with whom they worked. They further realized that the talents and skills of their colleagues had to be properly marshaled and focused if the effort was to succeed. Some aspects of their improvement efforts were not completely successful; but in each case there was enough success to generate energy and enthusiasm, which enabled their efforts to continue.

In this fastback I have presented you with a systematic way of looking at your management style and of comparing it with the style of high performers. It takes some time to use the various charts I have suggested for analyzing and carrying out a personal work plan, and it may be a while before you see results. But the long-term rewards are worth it. High performers are energized by seeing a good organization become a better one. Such energy is contagious; high performers beget other high performers. And in the school business, the rewards transcend those in other organizations, because the outcome is children and youth achieving their potential as human beings.

Appendix

Chart #1
My Core Values and Mission

1. Write what you believe to be your personal and professional core values — those that you will never compromise.

2. Write what you believe to be your value to the organization.

3. Write what you perceive others think is your value to the organization — your unique qualities or special attributes.

4. Write your personal mission statement.

Chart #2
Colleagues' Special Skills and
Their Value to the Organization

Name: _____

Position: _____

1. Special Skills:

2. Value to Organization:

3. Training Strategies:

Chart #3
Time Assessment Schedule

Day:

Activity	8am	9am	10am	11am	12pm	1pm	2pm	3pm	4pm
Planning									
Dictation									
Paperwork									
Telephone									
Meetings									
Travel									
Classroom Visits									
Plant Visits									
Teacher Conferences									
Student/Parent Conferences									
Teacher Evaluations									
Teacher Training									

Chart #4
Improvement Activity Analysis

Prior Week _____
Self-renewing activities:

Activities to improve individuals:

Activities to improve organization:

Next Week _____
Self-renewing activities:

Activities to improve individuals:

Activities to improve organization:

Chart #5
Personal Work Plan

Mission Statement:			
GOAL	ACTIVITIES	DATE	EXPECTED RESULTS

SOUTHERN NEW HAMPSHIRE UNIVERSITY

3 4676 00115 3789

Bibliography

Alward, Joseph F. *Alpha Chart*. Stockton, Calif.: Spectral Graphics Software, 1983.

Austin, Nancy, and Peters, Thomas. *A Passion for Excellence*. New York: Random House, 1985.

Barnard, Chester I. *The Functions of the Executive*. Cambridge, Mass.: Harvard University Press, 1968.

Bobbe, Richard, et al. *Work Planning for Action*. Stamford, Conn.: Schaeffer Associates, 1974.

Culligan, Matthew J.; Deakins, C. Suzanne; and Young, Arthur H. *Back to Basics Management*. New York: Facts on File, 1983.

Garfield, Charles. *Peak Performers*. New York: William Morrow, 1986.

Goodlad, John. *A Place Called School*. New York: McGraw-Hill, 1984.

Halberstam, David. *The Reckoning*. New York: William Morrow, 1986.

Kass, R.C., and Webster, William. *Rational Planning for Public Agencies*. Washington, D.C.: Washington Center for Metropolitan Studies, 1972.

Musashi, Miyamoto. *A Book of Five Rings*. Woodstock, N.Y.: Overlook Press, 1982.

Ouchi, William G. *The M-Form Society*. Reading, Mass.: Addison-Wesley, 1984.

Peters, Thomas J., and Waterman, Robert H., Jr. *In Search of Excellence*. New York: Harper & Row, 1982.

Sizer, Theodore. *Horace's Compromise*. Boston: Houghton Mifflin, 1984.

Walton, Mary. *The Deming Management Method*. New York: Dodd, Mead, 1986.